Praying from the

THIRD
DIMENSION

THE WORKBOOK

T h e   T a b e r n a c l e   o f   M o s e s

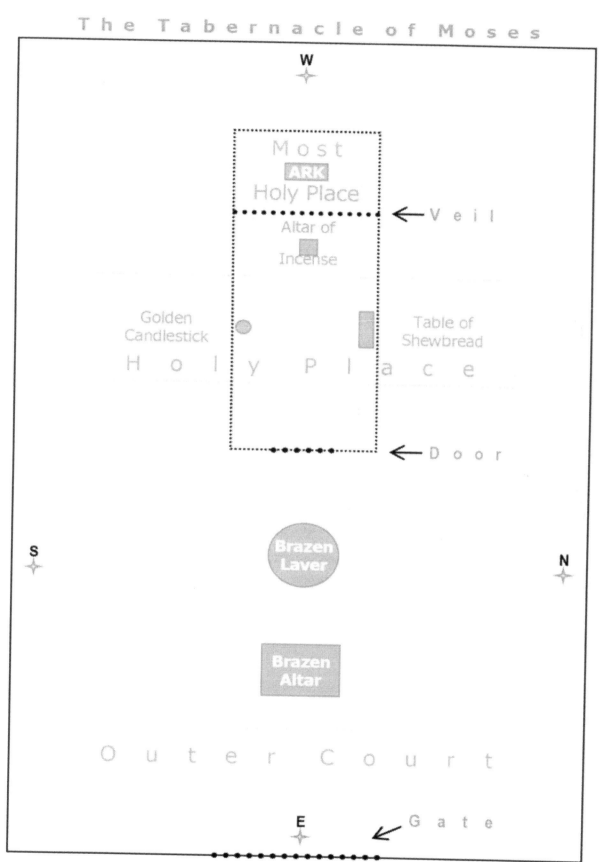

The Cross in the Tabernacle Furniture

The companion for this workbook is Praying From The Third Dimension THE REVISED EDITION by Dr. Juanita Bynum. It is highly recommended that you read "Praying From The Third Dimension" while completing this workbook. For this and all other ministry materials from Dr. Juanita Bynum, please log onto www.juanitabynum.com

Table Of Content

Preface Review
MY JOURNEY IN PRAYER

My mind reflects back on the beginning of my journey. Even as a child, I always enjoyed observing different levels of the anointing, and watching the Holy Ghost move upon powerful men and women of God. Of the many evangelists that I have seen in my lifetime, one in particular, Missionary Everett, stands out. Whenever our pastor called her to the podium, she would pray, and the anointing hit the room! She was mighty in the Spirit.

Having grown up in the Church of God in Christ, I went to conventions and watched ministers like Mother Elsee Shaw, a great intercessor of our time and Sister Kelly, an awesome intercessor who still ministers in prayer to this day; and of course, my grandmother, Doretha Bynum was one that I watched very closely and intently. Her prayer ministry boasted of the power and presence of God.

I remember standing in amazement as spiritual transitions would take place in these services, watching how an auditorium or building would be transformed into a sanctuary— people standing, praying, with a prayer leader on the microphone—and then suddenly, the whole atmosphere would shift. I could literally feel a "weight" descending upon the people. It would "sit" in the building, getting thicker and thicker, and then shift, turn again, and the room would fall into silence.

Slowly, the sounds of groaning and wailing, and the cries of those who were travailing in tears would begin to rise up to heaven. Then suddenly, heaven's door opened and God stepped down into the midst of His people. I would look around, amazed, at people's faces that confirmed their hearts and minds had embraced the Lord's answer. This was—and still is—an awesome sight.

People go to concerts, or to hear somebody preach, sing, or play an instrument— and these things can be incredible—but nothing compares to watching prayer in process. Prayer brings a right now result, entering into our Father's presence and experiencing all that He is.

History has seen many gifted ministers of God, but no one has ever mastered prayer. Some have mastered playing an instrument; others have mastered the art of preaching—but none can claim "mastery" over prayer. God is the only Master of it. He owns the eternal rights to prayer, and that is why it does not matter how many people have written books on this topic. God has and always will unfold something new.

Prayer is ongoing communion with God to the point that we begin to know His heart and mind. Can anyone fully, and completely, experience all that God is?

The process of prayer never ends, because God is eternal. He is the first, and the last, the Alpha and the Omega. This is why I believe **Luke 18:1** says, **"…men ought always to pray, and not to faint."** God has commanded us to pray without ceasing, because there will always be something that we need to learn about Him.

GOD CALLED ME TO THE NEXT LEVEL

As the years passed, and my mother attended conventions, I would always say, "Whatever you do, bring me back some prayer tapes." And she did. Listening to prayer cassettes became my favorite pastime. I would love hearing people like C.H. Mason, Mother Shaw, or Etheo Clemens pray. Then I came across Larry Lea's Could You Not Tarry One Hour? and once again, God transformed my ability to enter His presence.

God called me to the ministry of prayer in 1998. (I remember it well, because that was the year that I preached a message called "Refiner's Fire" at a conference hosted by Bishop T.D. Jakes.) I had fallen asleep downstairs on the couch in my den. At about 4:30 a.m., the sound of something hitting the floor jarred me to consciousness. Since I had been attacked many times by demonic forces that had entered a room (or had spiritual warfare in the middle of the night), I immediately sat up and began speaking in tongues, because I felt like this was yet another spiritual warfare.

I looked around, and then noticed a plaque that had fallen to the floor from the mantle. It had been a gift from a friend. It was a special gift to me because it spelled and described my name. I got up, put the plaque back in its place, and went back to sleep. Bam! It hit the floor again. When I got up this time, I said to myself, "Okay, I know that I set this plaque back up correctly; for it to keep falling off of the mantle, something is up." Upset, I started binding the enemy; because I felt that he was trying to mess with my name (the description on the plaque was so powerful).

Once again, I put the plaque back on the mantle, and went to sleep. A third time, it fell. When I woke up, I heard the Lord say, "I am calling you to prayer." Then He said, "Look at the clock." It was 5:00 a.m. God told me, "If you do not pray, this is what the enemy desires to do to the power of the name that I am establishing for you in the earth. He desires for you to hit the ground." Then He said, "Prayer, for you, is not going to be optional. It is mandatory. It is your lifestyle. You will not be able to survive the spiritual warfare that is coming against you, because of your assignment, if you do not pray."

That day, I started praying at 5:00 a.m. In fact, many mornings I did not even need an alarm—and I am not a morning person! Nevertheless, my eyes would automatically open at 5:00 a.m., like clockwork. Bam! I was awake, and I started having personal experiences with the Lord.

Much of what people see happening in my life right now was birthed out of intercession in 1998.

People may look at me and say, "The favor of God is on her life," or "The hand of God is with her," but the reality is that God revealed things to me in prayer, and I had to birth them out. I birthed out the nation. There were times that I was on my basement floor for hours, starting at 5:00 a.m.—not realizing how long I had been there! God would show me masses of people, and I would travail in prayer for hours. God was saying, "You are called to the nation long before you get to the nation. You are called to them long before you get to them. The reason they will be able to receive you is because you have already met in the Spirit realm."

Yes, I believe that the people I preach to now are those whom I have already called forth in the Spirit realm. God placed them in my loins. They were my "assignment" years before I stood before them in the natural! No, I do not believe that I am drawing a random crowd. People do not just hear about the name, Juanita Bynum, and come to hear me minister. God has already designated these people in the Spirit realm; they are part of my spiritual assignment.

When you begin to realize the power of prayer, how it governs and channels your future, then you will truly understand why you should pray.

Though Peter wavered, he was able to stand again because Jesus had said, **"But I have prayed especially for you [Peter], that your [own] faith may not fail..." Luke 22:32, (AMP)** Though Peter stumbled, he could not ultimately fail—because prayer had already gone up before him. The Holy Spirit said that Peter had not "watched and prayed" with Jesus in the Garden of Gethsemane, so he fell when his faith was tested. Yet ultimately, Jesus restored Him, because Peter's victory had already birthed out in prayer.

Prayer reaches into the future, stabilizes us, and seals our destination.

Prayer puts us in the position where Satan cannot cancel our destiny, because that prayer has already been answered! Things that you pray for now, that God will do in the future, cannot be altered...they have already been answered and sealed in the Holy Ghost!

Jesus had to agonize in prayer in the Garden of Gethsemane, because He already knew His spiritual assignment, but He had to break through the fleshly realm that did not want to submit to the assignment. The Bible says that He was **"slain from the foundation of the world" Rev. 13:8**, so Jesus was not slain on the cross! That is where the process was completed, where the manifestation took place from what had already been declared in heaven.

If Jesus agonized in prayer so that His flesh would not get in the way of the Spirit, then we need to pray just like He did. We must pray so the flesh realm does not hinder what God has already proclaimed that we are supposed to be, and have, in the Spirit realm.

When we agonize in prayer, our Spirit man leaps beyond the flesh realm! Always remember that everything you are going to be and do is connected to what you are praying right now. You do not get to the future, and then pray! Through my experiences in prayer, I have come to understand one thing. Everything that exists was first created in the Spirit realm, and then it is manifested in the flesh. The things that are happening in Christendom now in the flesh (worldly) realm, already existed in the Spirit realm.

When I realized that prayer was the key to my future, I began to spend every morning in prayer. The Lord also instructed me at that time to keep a prayer journal, so I began to write down the things that He would tell me. Every morning, I would pray and write down what God said.

Amazingly, I can read back through my prayer journals and see how God has brought these things to pass. It is a blessing when people say, "I have been praying for you," but there is nothing like seeing a manifestation of the glory of God that results from your own prayers! I had been praying since I became a Christian, here and there until that morning in 1998. I was what you would call an Outer Court prayer (we will get more into this later, as we study the three levels of prayer).

God was calling me to the third dimension of prayer, which means I started to spend unlimited time with Him. I have heard people say, "If you start out by praying 7 minutes a day, that will be okay; then move to 15 minutes a day, etc." When God called me to the third dimension of prayer, I prayed for hours! God gave me a time of day to pray when I did not have to rush my time with Him, because He wanted to begin to do things for me and through me. Supernaturally.

When I accepted this call, I began to see results. Things started to change in my life at a speed that was so rapid, it almost scared me. There were times I almost began to believe that I was going to die, but God was trying to help me understand that this is where He wanted me to live. He said, "The blessings that are now coming upon your life at this accelerated rate is how I desire for all of My people to live."

If He took me to the next level in prayer, He will do the same for you.

GOD BEGAN TO REVEAL HIS PATTERN

Over the last 3 years, the Lord began to deal with me about going "behind the veil." This new pattern steadily gained a significant, and unusual, influence in my heart and mind. After I had completed volume I of Morning Glory, I thought that the following year, we would release the next music CD, Morning Glory, volume II. This is when an unusual process began, and I did not see the pattern until later.

When we operate in the Spirit realm, we simply do what we are "led" to do, or have been arrested by the Lord to do—without taking time to examine the pattern of the Lord, how He works, and makes things happen. God does everything according to a pattern. He operates according to divine order. Many times, we do not pay attention to this when we are "flowing" in the Spirit.

As we learn to pay close attention to what God is doing, then we will see beyond the natural realm. In other words, something we may "naturally" have thought was an isolated incident is actually the beginning of something in the Spirit. Something that looks like it is just starting to happen could very well be coming to an end, while something else is in the middle stages of spiritual development. What you see and experience reflects where you are in God's pattern.

What am I trying to say? God's pattern, from the beginning, has been revealed through the Tabernacle of Moses. He gave specific instructions then, and He has continued to deal with the body of Christ according to the three stages of this pattern: the Outer Court, the Holy Place, and the Most Holy Place.

God's pattern of prayer also deals with our character, and as a result, our walk with Him. It never changes. For example, think about how our churches are built. There is usually an outer foyer that leads to the inner sanctuary. From there, you go to the altar.

In every sanctuary, the altar leads us into the presence of God. In the Tabernacle, God's manifest presence remained in the Most Holy Place, between the cherubim on the Ark. This "altar" is something that we have not been able to recreate, because it requires us to constantly repent and seek the Lord. We must prepare a place for His presence to "sit" in our earthly tabernacles. As I began to understand the pattern of the Lord, I realized why we are not effective in prayer. We do not move to the next level by living in obedience to God. He has already told us that we are to move from "faith to faith" and "glory to glory." **(Rom. 1:77, & 2 Cor. 3:18)** This means we have to apply faith in God, through prayer, to get to the next level of glory. We are "transformed" as we obey Him.

The first Morning Glory CD was called "Peace." was powerful, and though we experienced a little bit of warfare here and there, it was not "unbearable." So the next year, when the Lord told me that we were going to do volume II, I rushed to do it the same way. God had moved to another level, He impressed in my heart that I was to be still, so we released the small cassette, Be Still. I obeyed God, but I did not see the pattern. I did not realize God was doing something that would be "fitly joined together" with what He is doing in my life right now.

The next CD, Behind the Veil, went to another level. Initially, I thought God would give us songs that pertained to His divine presence and that would be that. One thing led to another, and it took us 3 years to complete a project that we thought would be finished in one.

Every time we received a song from the Lord, we would enter a new level of warfare.

In January 2000, we received the title cut, "Come Go with Me Behind The Veil," and my Pastor suffered a major stroke. The left side of his body was paralyzed, and we did not know where our church was headed. This thrust us into another level of prayer, which opened my eyes to the pattern of the Lord. God began to show me the 3 levels of prayer, according to the pattern of the Tabernacle: "Outer Court" prayer, "Holy Place" intercession, and abiding in the glory of God "behind the veil" in the Most Holy Place.

I had no idea that I would eventually write about it.

As I pressed past my usual personal prayer time, and the perception that I had "gotten in the loop" in developing my own method of prayer, I knew there was more. Even though I had been getting up every day to pray at 5:00 a.m., and was having awesome experiences with God, His presence was not "resting" on me continually. This is where I feel that you may be right now. You have had some awesome times in prayer, but other days you have felt like you cannot find your way into the presence of the Lord. When this happens, you decided to "just wait" on His presence—but really, you have wondered, "Where has it gone? Where is that awesome experience that I had a few days ago?" God has revealed to me that His awesome, divine presence can and should be something we experience every time we pray. It was never meant to happen randomly, or moment-to-moment.

Our greatest experience with the Lord in prayer comes when, knowingly or not, we have followed the pattern.

Many times, you do not recognize what you did in order to reach that new level in prayer. You just know on that day, it was different. You started out one way, turned and went another direction, and then the "weighty" presence of God came and "sat" in your midst. Suddenly, you were in a supernatural realm with God, one that you had never experienced. You were able to embrace all that He had for you—there were no problems—only answers. Then the next day, you try, but cannot repeat the pattern. It happens over and over again.

God wants us to understand that there is a pattern, a way into His presence. He is calling us to press beyond having an "awesome experience." He wants us to take the time to observe and understand how He works in prayer.

If we understand His pattern, answered prayer can be an everyday reality.

God wants us to know—beyond the shadow of a doubt— that we have touched His throne every time we pray. He wants us to be assured that He hears our prayers, and will answer us.

Prayer becomes a chore when you do not understand the process. When you are "all thumbs" in the presence of the Lord, He may be calling you to another level. God does not want you to be unaware of the enemy's "devices." (**2 Cor. 2:11**) These devices do not have to be evil attacks that come against you. They can come when you do not recognize and submit to the pattern that will bring you into God's presence. Thus, you can become deceived by the enemy. Realize this—Satan is offended because we have accepted Christ, but he is not overwhelmed in this offense…because he knows that we will not go deeper in the Spirit without learning the pattern of prayer.

Prayer is the key to our lifestyle, and it is the key to discovering new levels in God. Therefore, we cannot fail to pray.

Prayer is the answer to every situation we will ever encounter. Prayer not only changes things, it changes everything, from the end to the beginning. **Matthew 9:37– 38 says,**

"Then He said to His disciples, The harvest is indeed plentiful, but the laborers are few. So pray to the Lord of the harvest to force out and thrust laborers into His harvest." (AMP)

Jesus did not say to thrust laborers into the vineyard; He said that laborers would be thrust into the harvest through people who pray! It has already happened! For example, when you plant and water seeds in a garden, and till the ground, you can wait expectantly for a harvest. So Jesus does not thrust praying people into the tilling process, He thrusts people that pray into a harvest!

When you pray, you come into the manifestation of what already exists! You are thrust into the end result…the finished process!

Remember that everything with God is already "finished," so when you pray, you are not trying to find out how God is going to do His work, you are entering into His finished work. Many times, you do not know that His work is completed because you are too far from Him. Your communication with Him is hindered, because you have not moved from level-to-level in obedience to His Word.

Everything that you need, everything you desire, as we begin this journey back to prayer, has already been "accomplished." You only need to go to the Spirit realm to find the completed harvest, and by way of your physical being, bring that harvest back to the earthly realm. You have to press through the Outer Court into the Holy Place, and then beyond, to the Most Holy Place—where the presence of God lives eternally. You are the chariot that brings the end result of God back into the earth realm.

If someone were to call me and say, "I have a million dollars for you," and they live on the west side of town, and I live on the east side of town, the only thing between me getting the money is transportation. It is the same with the things of God. You have to believe what He says and God uses your mouth, body, and spirit man to transport everything He is and does back to the natural realm. At every level that you obey, God grants a deeper level of grace and revelation. When you follow God to the third dimension of prayer, you become His means of transportation to receive what He has already "completed" for you, your family, your church, and every area of your life.

So, why not go back to prayer?

Questions

1a.) What are "Spiritual transitions" that can take place during a church service? Have you experienced a "Spiritual transition" in a service?

_____

_____

_____

1b.) As described in this Preface, what transpired prior to heaven's doors being opened?

_____

_____

_____

1c.) What is God's expectation of us as it relates to prayer?

_____

_____

_____

1d.) Is Prayer an art that can be "mastered" (please explain)?

_____

_____

_____

1e.) Who owns the only rights to the "mastery" of Prayer?

_____

_____

_____

Composition Questions

1. In 1998 my life of Intercession was birthed out of a clearly defined encounter with God. Can you recall when and/or how your prayer life of intercession was birthed?

_____

_____

_____

2. According to Luke 22:32, Peter wavered, but was able to "get up again", why? And can we replicate the same?

_____

_____

_____

3. What are some things that have the ability to cause you to waver in your prayer life?

_____

_____

_____

4. Jesus finished His assignment at the cross, but according to Rev. 13:8, the process began before the cross, please elaborate more on this scripture as it relates to the assignment of Jesus?

_____

_____

_____

5. In order to fulfill your God-given assignment of Prayer, what should be key components?

_____

_____

_____

6. Prayer instructions from God have a "pattern" if we are obedient and follow His leading. What would you say is your God given "prayer pattern" developed out of your obedience to His instructions?

_____

_____

_____

7. What scripture(s) can be referenced as it relates to the difference between instructions in Prayer versus the application of Prayer?

_____

_____

_____

8. When does Prayer become a "chore"? When...

_____

_____

_____

List 3 things that Prayer is according to the description in this section, and provide scripture reference?

a. _____

b. _____

c. _____

Selah

Pause, and Calmly Think of That

MEDITATION

Upon the Completion of the preface please write your most intimate thoughts about this chapter

_____

_____

_____

_____

_____

_____

_____

_____

_____

_____

_____

_____

_____

_____

_____

_____

Introduction

OUR JOURNEY TOGETHER

In going back to prayer, we are starting a journey that will ultimately take us to the Most Holy Place. In terms of this series, I am presenting each level of prayer in a separate volume. In this first volume, I talk about the Outer Court, or the introduction to prayer and intercession. Volume II goes into the Holy Place and the last volume will take us into the Most Holy Place, or the Holy of Holies.

How quickly you apply these truths to your life will determine how long your journey will be. In order for you to enter intercession on the third dimensional level, you will need to "do" what you read in each chapter every single day. God has required this of me, and He will require the same of anyone whom He has called to intercession.

You will notice that I have used Moses' Tabernacle as our model for the life of prayer. I have not attempted to cover every detail of this Tabernacle, because it contains many significant types and shadows. Instead, I am focusing on the areas that God has dealt with me as it relates to intercession, both from the scriptures and during my times in prayer with Him. I am sharing with you from my life, and how God has brought me into His Most Holy Place through prayer, intercession, and sanctification.

Each chapter has a "Selah" section at the end, with questions for you to answer, followed by blank journal pages for you to begin your journey in prayer. Yes, God will speak to you! **John 10:27** says that you are His sheep, you can hear His voice.

I want you to take time in each chapter, study the scriptures, prayerfully answer every question, and seek God to hear what He has to say. Write your answers on the journal pages; as well as what He reveals to you in prayer. This marks the beginning of your journey. I encourage you to buy a journal and write everything down that God speaks to you.

As you move from personal prayer in this volume (into volumes that follow), you will begin to hear God's voice more clearly. When God begins to use you to intercede for others, you must be able to hear His instructions about how to pray, as well as how He expects you to live in His presence. You must walk the path of prayer on a personal level before God can use you to effectively intercede for others.

I recommend that you get a copy of the Kingdom Principles passport booklet. You will be able to use it during your prayer times, or anytime that you need to know what the Word says concerning a situation. Over-and-above this, you need to make sure that you are studying the Bible on your own each day, because without it, you cannot be shaped into the image of God. If you do not operate like your Father, how can you do His work?

Now I understand, more than ever, why **James 5:16** says, **"...The earnest (heartfelt, continued) prayer of a righteous man makes tremendous power available [dynamic in its working]." (AMP) Psalm 34:15–20** adds,

"The eyes of the Lord are toward the [uncompromisingly] righteous and His ears are open to their cry. The face of the Lord is against those who do evil, to cut off the remembrance of them from the earth. When the righteous cry for help, the Lord hears, and delivers then out of all their distress and troubles. The Lord is close to those who are of a broken heart and saves such as are crushed with sorrow for sin and are humbly and thoroughly penitent. Many evils confront the [consistently] righteous, but the Lord delivers him out of them all. He keeps all his bones; not one of them is broken."
(AMP)

Do you want God to hear your prayers?
Keep reading. The truth is going to set you free!

Remember this book is first and foremost, teaching tool— so if I repeat something that I have said before, in order to move to the next point—bear with me. I want to make sure that you understand exactly what the Holy Ghost is saying, and see the pattern that He is establishing.

I believe that God is speaking a word for this season and hour. We must hear the Word, and do what it says, or we will not move to the next level.

THE TRUTH ABOUT THE LORD'S PRAYER

As I became obedient to the Lord in fasting, He began to show me how the Lord's Prayer is actually an introduction to prayer for the immature Christian. It is a starting place. Some believers have been stuck praying this pattern for years! It is supposed to lead us to another level in God; we are not supposed to stay There Just like the Outer Court in Moses' Tabernacle, we must "move through" this prayer on our journey to a deeper relationship with God, and deeper revelation. Remember, when Jesus gave this model prayer, He was talking to people that had not heard the voice of God for over 400 years—so He told them something to get them started. They were at the beginning of their journey. They were supposed to grow from there.

If you are called of God to become an intercessor; then the Lord's Prayer is simply an outline, a table of contents. It points to things that you must look into more deeply. It shows a path that you must follow to reach the conclusion of God. What was God's conclusion to me about intercessory prayer? As I sought Him, He said, "If you are going to become an intercessor, then you must go back and look at the pattern of how to become an intercessor," which led me beyond the Lord's Prayer to the Tabernacle.

ARE WE PRAYING ACCORDING TO GOD'S PATTERN?

It is important that we pray, but it is vital that we pray correctly. Are we experiencing effective prayer, according to God's pattern? If God set a pattern, then He expects us to pray "decently and in order" **1 Cor. 14:40**, in harmony with His plan. This is how He wants everything done in His Church!

If we fall out of the pattern for prayer, we can easily begin to pray according to our emotions, which are fruitless, or according to our logical mind, which leads to a spirit of control and witchcraft. You can pray and get an emotional release, o r you can pray to ease your mind, but are you praying according to God's pattern? Praying according to God's will has nothing to do with what you think, or how you feel.

James 3:17 says,

"But the wisdom from above is first of all pure (undefiled); then it is peace-loving, courteous (considerate, gentle). [It is willing to] yield to reason, full of compassion and good fruits; it is wholehearted and straightforward, impartial and unfeigned (free from doubts, wavering, and insincerity). And the harvest of righteousness (of conformity to God's will in thought and deed) is [the fruit of the seed] sown in peace by those who work for and make peace [in themselves and in others, that peace which means concord, agreement, and harmony between individuals, with undisturbedness, in a peaceful mind free from fears and agitating passions and moral conflicts]."
(AMP)

If you are living according to God's Word, and praying according to His pattern, God will begin to lead you out of personal prayer and into the deeper realm of intercession. He will lead you to pray according to what is in His heart, not yours. You will begin to pray from a heavenly perspective, not according to earthly wisdom.

On the other hand, if you are not living for God or praying according to His pattern, you will be praying one thing, and thinking another. You will be confessing one thing, and feeling something totally different. There will be constant conflict inside of you. Therefore, You will not be set free, and neither will anybody else. After God had called me to pray at my church (I now lead Tuesday morning prayer), He began, slowly and surely, veal the problems we face while we pray. He showed me that when we do not understand the pattern of prayer, we cannot consistently attack a certain realm and gain ground. We cannot consistently come into His presence to receive direction. As Paul said, we end up "beating the air" with our fists, **1 Cor. 9:26, (AMP).** We end up praying with no vision, or direction, and will soon perish. **(Prov. 29:18)**

I have been in church almost all of my life, so I know that if God revealed this to me, you are probably experiencing the same problem; and I promise, if you are truly seeking God in prayer, the revelation He has given in this book will change your life. I know that my prayer life will never be the same, and I prophesy to you that as you embrace this word of the Lord, your prayer life will be "transported" to the next level.

I have prayed that this book would be put into the hands of people in prisons, or in hospitals. I have also prayed that it would fall into the hands of those who do not know the Lord, or how to pray. If this is you, keep reading. Keep turning the pages, and you will meet God. Not only this, you will come to know Him intimately, and hear His voice in your spirit. My friend, God has made sure that you picked up this book, so that He can set you free!

If on the other hand, you are a mature Christian, or maybe you are a Jewish follower of the Messiah, keep reading. God has led me to our spiritual roots. He has unfolded the mysteries of His Word to me as it concerns prayer and intercession. Keep reading. Let us take this journey together.

Questions

1. What are the three levels of prayer according to each volume?

_____

_____

_____

2. What is the one requirement in determining how long your journey will be in understanding prayer?

_____

_____

_____

3. In this section, prayer transitioning is described as a walk; however, we are on a what?

_____

_____

_____

4. When we pray, it is important to know the direction you are going as well as the destination. What is your place of destination for this book?

_____

_____

_____

3. NAME THE ATTRIBUTES OF THE WISDOM OF GOD, AND HOW EACH ONE APPLIES TO YOU.

a. _____

_____

_____

b. _____

_____

_____

c. _____

_____

_____

d. _____

_____

_____

e. _____

_____

_____

f.

_____

_____

_____

g.

_____

_____

_____

h.

_____

_____

_____

Composition Question

1. How are we shaped into the image of God?

_____

_____

_____

2. How does prayer avail much?

_____

_____

_____

3. The pattern of The Lord's Prayer is used as a tool to help us do what?

_____

_____

_____

4. How long had it been since the people heard the voice of God?

_____

_____

_____

5. What are the dangers in not following pattern which God has set?

_____

_____

_____

MEDITATION

Selah

Pause, and Calmly Think of That

Upon the Completion of The Introduction please write your most intimate thoughts about this chapter

_____

_____

_____

_____

_____

_____

_____

_____

_____

_____

_____

_____

_____

_____

Chapter One
THE GATE REVIEW

INTRODUCTION TO PRAYER

When you go to a tailor, he takes measurements
and then cuts out a pattern to fit your body. If he cuts it the wrong way, according
to the wrong measurements, you will not be able to wear the outfit. It will not fit.
Though the outfit may be beautiful, it will be useless.

It is the same with God's presence. If we do not structure our prayer life according
to the pattern that He has "cut," then He will not be able to step in to our prayers!
He cannot commune with us. God cannot step into your time of prayer, unless it
has been structured according to the pattern that He has established. Why? Like I
said before, He is the master of prayer. God is the only one that knows the
measurements of His Spirit. **(Rom. 8:27)**

So the first step in your journey to third dimensional prayer is to look for the
pattern by which we are to enter the presence of the Lord. You must know that
answered prayer is not luck, nor does it happen by chance. Look back at the times
that you have prayed and received an answer.

Most likely, you will discover that you actually prayed according to God's
pattern, so you got God's results. There are times when God sovereignly
seems to answer an "out of pattern" prayer. If He does, then God is God! He
can choose to act after the counsel of His own will. In other words, as He said to
Moses,

**"…I will proclaim My name, THE LORD, before you; for I will be gracious
to whom I will be gracious, and will show mercy and loving-kindness on
whom I will show mercy and loving-kindness."**
Exodus 33:19, (AMP)

Who are we to question God? We must simply learn to come into His presence,

"Let the wicked forsake his way and the unrighteous man his thoughts; and let him return to the Lord, and He will have love, pity, and mercy for him, and to our God, for He will multiply to him His abundant pardon. For My thoughts are not your thoughts, neither are your ways My ways, says the Lord. For as the heavens are higher than the earth, so are My ways higher than your ways and My thoughts than your thoughts. For as the rain and snow come down from the heavens, and return not there again, but water the earth and make it bring forth and sprout, that it may give seed to the sower and bread to the eater, so shall My word be that goes forth out of My mouth: it shall not return to Me void [without producing any effect, useless], but it shall accomplish that which I please and purpose, and it shall prosper in the thing for which I sent it." Isaiah 55:7–11, (AMP)

Questions

There are times when you are not looking for a pattern, times when you do not know what you are actually doing during your time of prayer and you will either enter into communion with God, or you will not. Sometimes you get results, and other times, you do not. Then the frustration begins, and it's not long before you stop praying altogether. This is a tool of the enemy. He wants to discourage you from pressing into God, and hinder God's purpose for your life.

1. What will prevent God from stepping into our prayers?

   _____

   _____

   _____

2. What is the first step into your journey to third dimensional prayers?

   _____

   _____

   _____

3. **Will God ever choose to answer an out of pattern prayer?**

_____

_____

_____

4. **What does the word Sovereign mean?**

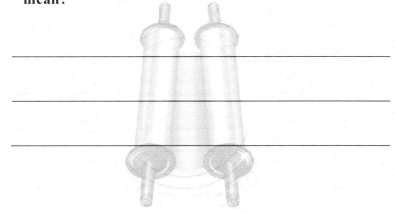

_____

_____

_____

RETURNING TO THE BEGINNING

As mentioned before, Jesus gave us the Lord's Prayer
to begin our journey into the presence of God. It is our divine table of contents. Let us look more closely at **Matthew 6:9–13**,

> **"After this manner therefore, pray ye: Our Father which art in heaven, Hallowed be thy name. Thy kingdom come. Thy will be done in earth, as it is in heaven. Give us this day our daily bread. And forgive us our debts, as we forgive our debtors. And lead us not into temptation, but deliver us from evil: For thine is the kingdom, and the power, and the glory, forever. Amen."**

There are times when you are not looking for a pattern, times when you do not know what you are actually doing during your time of prayer and you will either enter into communion with God, or you will not. Sometimes you get results, and other times, you do not. Then the frustration begins, and it's not long before you stop praying altogether. This is a tool of the enemy. He wants to discourage you from pressing into God, and hinder God's purpose for your life.

1. **What is the difference between one who prays and one who intercedes?**

   _____

   _____

   _____

2. **The Lord's prayer starts with worship to God the Father. What are other names given to God?**

_____

_____

_____

3. **What is the importance of submitting your will to God's will?**

_____

_____

_____

4. **Define the term "daily bread."**

_____

_____

_____

5. **What is meant by maintenance portion of the scripture?**

_____

_____

_____

6. **Who does the Kingdom belong to?**

_____

_____

_____

7. List the two key indicators from The Lord's prayer—
    with the exception of "thy Kingdom come"— that the
    Kingdom belongs ONLY to God.

_____

_____

_____

Unfolding the pattern

1. Where is the entry cafe?

_____

_____

_____

2. Name the items in the Outer Court.

_____

_____

_____

3. Name the items in the Holy Place.

_____

_____

_____

_____

4. Name the item in the <u>most</u> holy place.

_____

_____

_____

The Gate to the Outer Court

1. Who established the
   Tabernacle?

_____

_____

_____

2. What was the wall built with?

_____

_____

_____

3. **Why was the color white?**

_____

_____

_____

4. **After the camps were set up, how were the people situated?**

_____

_____

_____

5. **Why did everyone have to enter at the same gate?**

_____

_____

_____

6. **What were the colors of the gate?**

_____

_____

_____

7. **What did the colors represent?**

_____

_____

_____

8. **What scripture confirms this?**

_____

_____

_____

9. **Since Jesus is the way to the Father, the café is the symbol of what?**

_____

_____

_____

10. **How must we enter this gate?**

_____

_____

_____

You Must Be Saved

1. Does God hear a sinner's prayer?

   _____

   _____

2. What must your first prayer be?

   _____

   _____

   _____

3. According to what scripture? (In reference to the previous question.)

   _____

   _____

   _____

The Perfect High Priest

1. Why did God decide to send us the "perfect" High Priest?

   _____

   _____

   _____

2. **Why did God have to predetermine the works of Christ?**

_____

_____

_____

3. **Is there a way that the priesthood in the Old Testament could be changed?**

_____

_____

_____

4. **Why did Jesus come after the order of Melchizedek? What did it mean?**

_____

_____

_____

5. **What is the whole purpose of cancelling the old order?**

_____

_____

_____

6. **Can Jesus' priesthood ever be changed? Why or why not?**

_____

_____

_____

Now do you see why you must not only identify with the 4 works (colors) of Christ (in the Gate), but receive and accept them into your own life? To enter prayer, even this first stage, you must begin with Christ…the Perfect High Priest.

The Power Of The Gate

1. **Jesus is the way, and there is no way outside of Him to the Father? Share the scriptures that support this statement. Explain this significance based on the power of "The GATE."**

    _____

    _____

    _____

2. **What kind of prayer gets the job done?**

    _____

    _____

    _____

3. **Why did Peter go to prison?**

    _____

    _____

    _____

4. **What caused an angel to appear inside the prison?**

    _____

    _____

    _____

5. **Was Peter conscious of what was being done by the angel? Why?**

_____

_____

_____

6. **How does the gate swinging open connect with the works of Jesus?**

_____

_____

_____

7. **Would you say that because of Peter's conversion, the opening of the gate on its own accord was prophetically connected to the original gate of the Tabernacle? Discuss why.**

_____

_____

_____

Composition Questions

(These questions are constructed for open discussions)

1. In order to have God "step into" our Prayers, we need to do the following?

2. What does this chapter say is our 1st step in this journey to the Third Dimension of Prayer?

3. Isaiah 55:7 gives us a patterned process to His presence. Can you share key elements that most reside in your spirit?

4. Matthew 6:9-13 talks about one of the most familiar Prayer's in the scripture. What is it called and for whom was it created?

5. Concerning topics discussed thus far, evaluate where you believe you are in your process of Prayer?

Selah

Pause, and Calmly Think of That

MEDITATION

Upon the Completion of Chapter One please write your most intimate thoughts about this chapter

Chapter Two
THE OUTER COURT REVIEW

THE EARLY STAGES OF PRAYER

God is constantly moving; He is always in transition. So when you get into the Outer Court, though it is the place that He wants you to begin in prayer, He demands that you do not remain there. You have entered His courts through the Gate of Jesus Christ, but He wants you to go deeper. The perfect example is when the children of Israel left Egypt. They started their journey by way of the wilderness, which was actually a place of blessing until they stayed there too long. This "blessed" place soon became the place of curses.

This leads us to the third step, following God's pattern of prayer.

In order to pass through Outer Court praying, you have to go through every stage that leads to the other side. Many of us enter into the courts of the Lord and embrace "religion," so we never going deeper into His presence. The Outer Court was established when God set the initial boundaries for the Tabernacle in **Exodus 27:9–15 & 17–18**. This corresponds to the initial conversion experience. Anybody and everybody that asks Jesus to come into their hearts can come into the Outer Court. It is a place of washing and repentance—a place we enter with thanksgiving for what He has done.

The Outer Court was also a place that was lit by the natural sunlight. So, though you are being offered eternal light through the plan of salvation, at this point, you are not given eternal revelation. You are still in natural light. If you remain in the Outer Court, though you are saved, you will constantly be exposed to natural elements— fleshly opinions, earthly circumstances—everything that goes on in the natural. You will stay in a place where you are constantly forced to accept the ways and conversations of mortal men.

In Israel, everybody gathered in the Outer Court. Conversations went on about what everybody thought about God, and what they thought about everything else, but if you want to go deeper in the things of the Spirit, you have to keep pressing through. Remember, when the Israelites murmured— complained to each other, talked amongst each other about what God was doing—they got delayed. It stopped their progress. Judgment came. Don't let Outer Court chatter hinder your prayers!

You have to remember that you are on a journey to the Most Holy Place, via the Holy Place, where only a priest can enter. Everybody could come into the Outer Court, but not the Holy Place, and certainly not the Holy of Holies.

When you remain an Outer Court person that prays, nothing about you is consistent. For example, Outer Court people pray "whenever." They pray in emergencies; when something terrible happens and it looks like they are going to be devastated, they cry out to God. Outer Court prayers stay in a "praise mode." They admire God, but they never come into relationship with Him. So, they never receive the revelation of His heart, and what God desires to do in the earth.

Outer Court pray-ers never get to the stage, "Thy kingdom come…" because they are saying, "I am saved, I know God, I honor God." They never pass through the courts into intercession, because they do not know God well enough to agonize in prayer on His behalf. Outer Court prayers are focused on washing, cleansing, and material things. They are always saying, "Give me…I need…" and not Lord, here I am, what is it that you need?

Questions

1. The Early Stages of Prayer

(1a.) Based on this book, we must move through the Outer court. How do you navigate this process through to the Inner court?

_____

_____

_____

(1b.) How does your lifestyle reflect your spiritual citizenship?

_____

_____

_____

(1c.) According to Exo. 29:9-15, what were the boundaries?

_____

_____

_____

(1d.) Outer court PRAYING requires what?

_____

_____

_____

(1e.) Many enter into the courts & never gain a relationship, WHY?

_____

_____

_____

2. You Are Not of This World

(2a.) Share your interpretation of Eternal light versus the Natural light offered to all who enter the outer courts?

_____

_____

_____

(2b.) Because of your revelation some things are no longer a temptation. Where and when does this tend to happen?

_____

_____

_____

(2c.) Why must we confess our sins?

_____

_____

_____

(2d.) What prohibits you from receiving divine revelation?

_____

_____

_____

3. You Cannot Stay In the Natural Light

(3a.) What two areas must you go through in order to get to the Holy Place?

_____

_____

_____

(3b.) What is the danger of praying by divine revelation?

_____

_____

_____

(3c.) What are the benefits of spiritual maturity?

_____

_____

(3d.) Name two reasons why we must get to maturity?

_____

_____

_____

(3e.) Whoever keeps the temple in order does what for the Word of God? Why? What scripture illustrates how to tap into the third realm?

_____

_____

_____

It has been noted that a person who remains steadfast can change anything.

4. A Glimpse of Glory

(4a.) Are we supposed to be held at simply experiencing the residue of His glory? Explain.

_____

_____

_____

(4b.) How are we held at simply experiencing the residue of the glory versus the third dimension, Most Holy Place, encounter of His glory?

_____

_____

_____

Questions continued

(These questions are constructed for open discussions)

1. Where does God always desire that we go in prayer?

_____

_____

_____

2. What are the transitions of the Holy Courts and what is our entrance gate?

_____

_____

_____

3. What scriptures refer to the initial boundaries for the Tabernacle?

_____

_____

_____

4. Who is welcome in the "Outer Courts" and what is provided for all who enter?

_____

_____

_____

5. There are several things that are not provided in the "Outer Courts". Discuss some things that are not provided in the "Outer Courts"?

_____

_____

_____

6. In this chapter, what examples were used of things that could hinder and/or delay your prayers? (Please provide scripture context)

_____

_____

_____

7. List 3 examples of Outer Court" prayers? (Meaning what do these prayers sound like or ask for?)

_____

_____

_____

8. The "Outer Court" is the _____
step into the _____   _____
It is intended for you to not remain.

Composition Questions
The Outer Court The Early Stages of Prayer | Ex.27:9–15

Have you been consistent in approaching God through the Gate of Jesus Christ (and His 4 works), and entering His courts with thankfulness and praise? What has changed in your heart, and life, since becoming consistently thankful to God? Has He started to lead you in a new direction? Journal your thoughts.

Does your life reflect being an ambassador for Christ? Has the Lord begun to reveal areas of your life that need to be renewed? Write them down. Read Hebrews 6:1–12. Thank God for giving you "faith and patience" to inherit every promise He has for you, and for your divine destiny. Write down what happens after you quiet yourself before Him in prayer.

Since you have started following God's pattern of prayer, have any "natural elements," like anger, gossip, difficult circumstances, etc., hindered you from spending time with God and going deeper in the Word? Take these experiences to God, ask Him for wisdom (for each one), and then lay your burdens at His feet. Write down what you receive from Him in prayer, and begin to move forward again.

Are you stuck in the "praise section" of prayer? Do you keep slipping back into sin? Go and "confess your fault" to a "righteous" man or woman (like your pastor…), so that God can deliver you, and get you back on course in prayer. Write in your journal about this experience, and thank God for His faithfulness.

Are you starting to see and experience the results of consistent prayer? Look back in your journal to when you began. Let God lead you through the pages, then write what He revealed to you on this journey.

Are you ready to leave the elementary things of God? Are you ready undergo the first stage of preparation for intercessory prayer? Update your list of things that (God has revealed) need to change in your heart and life. Read the Bible and find out what it says concerning these areas; ask God to lead you to the Brazen Laver.

MEDITATION

Selah

Pause, and Calmly Think of That

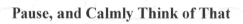

Upon the Completion Of Chapter Two please write your most intimate thoughts about this chapter

_____

_____

_____

_____

_____

_____

_____

_____

_____

_____

_____

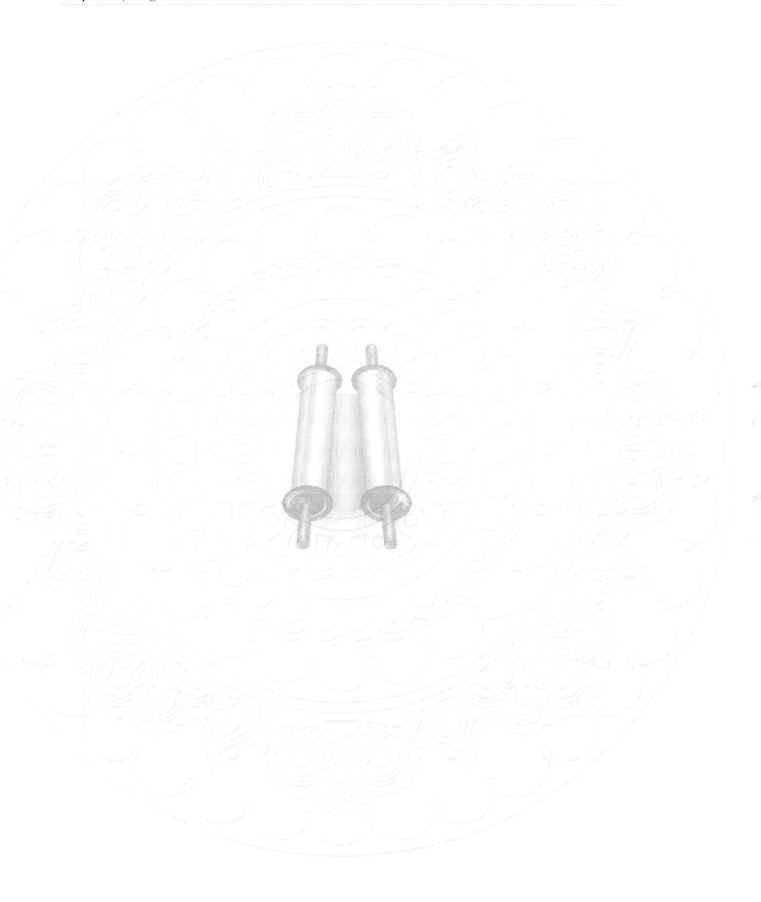

Chapter Three
THE BRAZEN LAVER REVIEW

THE PLACE OF WASHING

As you go deeper into the Outer Court, just passed the Brazen Altar, you encounter the first stage in this third step of the pattern of prayer—the Brazen Laver. Let me review. You have passed through the Gate that represents the 4 works of Jesus Christ: His righteousness, divinity (coming down from heaven to earth), kingship, and His ultimate sacrifice on the Cross. As He draws you deeper into His presence, you begin to experience the manifestation of these works—so you enter His courts in prayer, every day, praising and thanking God for what He has already done.

The Brazen Laver is the first place God will lead you in prayer. It represents the first piece of furniture in the Tabernacle, and the first part of God's nature that begins to embrace your life. It is your first stage of preparation to become an intercessor. **Exodus 30:19–21** says,

"For Aaron and his sons shall wash their hands and their feet thereat: when they go into the tabernacle of the congregation, they shall wash with water that they die not; or when they come near to the altar to minister, to burn offering made by fire unto the Lord: so shall they wash their hands and their feet, that they die not…"

All priests were required to wash before performing any ministry-function, so this tells us that prayer is not supposed to stay on the personal level. You are to pass through the "personal level" of prayer through the cleansing, so that you can begin to pray for others. If you are thinking, "I am not a priest." Think again. You are a priest, and if you are saved, God is going to begin a work in you that starts at the Brazen Laver.

"So be done with every trace of wickedness (depravity, malignity) and all deceit and insincerity (pretense, hypocrisy) and grudges (envy, jealousy) and slander and evil speaking of every kind. Like newborn babies you should crave (thirst

for, earnestly desire) the pure (unadulterated) spiritual milk, that by it you may be nurtured and grow unto [completed] salvation, since you have [already] tasted the goodness and kindness of the Lord. Come to Him [then, to that] Living Stone which men tried and threw away, but which is chosen [and] precious in God's sight. [Come] and, like living stones, be yourselves built [into] a spiritual house, for a holy (dedicated, consecrated) priesthood, to offer up [those] spiritual sacrifices [that are] acceptable and pleasing to God through Jesus Christ."
1 Peter 2:1–5, (AMP)

In other words, you have already tasted the goodness of God (through salvation) at the Gate, so now you are a priest—and God is about to dedicate and consecrate you unto Him. Unlike the five-fold ministry gifts in **Ephesians 4:11** (i.e., apostle, prophet, evangelist, pastor, and teacher), prayer has been given to "all men." You do not have to function in the five-fold ministry to pray. You are a priest, and no matter what you do in the church, or how old you are in Christ, God has called you to pray, every day. **Luke 18:1** says, **"…men ought always to pray, and not to faint…"**

2 Cor 7:1 says, **"Having therefore these promises, dearly beloved, let us cleanse ourselves from all filthiness of the flesh and spirit, perfecting holiness in the fear of God."**

Ephesians 5:26 says, **"Let no man deceive you with vain words: for because of these things cometh the wrath of God upon the children of disobedience."**

James 4:8 says, **"Draw nigh to God, and he will draw nigh to you. Cleanse your hands, ye sinners; and purify your hearts, ye double minded."**

Since prayer is not just a personal relationship with God, but also a ministry, before you can minister on any level— to yourself, someone else, or unto the Lord— you have to wash first. You cannot minister unless you have been "prepared" by God. **Ephesians 5:22–27** says,

"Wives, be subject (be submissive and adapt yourselves) to your own husbands as [a service] to the Lord. For the husband is head of the wife as Christ is the Head of the church, Himself the Savior of [His] body. As the church is subject to Christ, so let wives also be subject in everything to their husbands. Husbands, love your wives, as Christ loved the church and gave Himself up for her, so that He might sanctify her, having cleansed her by the washing of water with the Word, that He might present the church to Himself

in glorious splendor, without spot or wrinkle or any such things [that she might be holy and faultless]." (AMP)

In the natural, this is speaking to husbands and wives, but in the Spirit realm, it paints a picture of the cleansing every believer must undergo as the bride of Christ. Jesus gave up His life so that we would be sanctified, "…having cleansed her by the washing of water with the Word."

So as soon as you get into the Outer Court, the Lord is going to lead you straight to the Brazen Laver because He has already given Himself up so that you could be made righteous.

As you wash, you are stripping off the "old (unregenerate) self"—your flesh—according to **Colossians 3:9** (AMP), which cannot go to the next level of prayer. **John 6:63** says,

"It is the Spirit Who gives life [He is the Life-giver]; the flesh conveys no benefit whatever [there is no profit in it]. The words (truths) that I have been speaking to you are spirit and life." (AMP)

Questions

1. The Place of Washing

(1a.) Why must the brazen laver be the first stop?

_____

_____

_____

(1b.) In the process of traveling through the courts many times are you called to wash?

_____

_____

_____

(1c.) What is the penalty when this law is disobeyed?

_____

_____

_____

(1d.) According to John 13:9-11, why did Jesus wash the feet of the disciples?

_____

_____

_____

(1e.) Why have we become priests?

_____

_____

_____

(1f.) As the priest, explain how Ephesians 5:22-27 connects to our priesthood and the church?

_____

_____

_____

(1g.) Why did the priests burn the flesh and why?

_____

_____

_____

2. A Perfect Construction

(2a.) What was unique about the construction of the Brazen Laver?

_____

_____

_____

(2b.) Why was it made from bronze?

_____

_____

_____

(2c.) What were the measurements of the laver?

_____

_____

_____

(2d.) Why wasn't there wood in it?

_____

_____

_____

(2e.) What does wood represent?

_____

_____

_____

3. *A Perfect Reflection*

(3a.)   **Who provided the mirrors at the door?**

_____

_____

_____

(3b.)   **Where was another place a reflection was seen?**

_____

_____

_____

(3c.)   **According to 1 Peter 2:1, list 3 things we are told to be done with in order for the "completed" work of salvation to continue?**

_____

_____

_____

(3d.)   **According to James 1;22-25, why is it dangerous to hear the cleansing Word and not obey it?**

_____

_____

_____

4. *A Perfect Communion*

(4a.) Hebrews 4:12-14 asserts four things about the power of the Word, what are they?

_____

_____

_____

(4b.)Perfect communion with Jesus means walking through every stage of intercession. What does that process look like for you?

_____

_____

_____

(4c.) Why is it important to follow Jesus on this course?

_____

_____

_____

(4d.) How do we commune with Christ?

_____

_____

_____

(4e.) What does the bread and wine represent?

_____

_____

_____

(4f.) How do we demonstrate the works that He has already done?

_____

_____

_____

5. *You Can Not Stay At The Laver*

(5a.) Remaining at the Brazen Laver prevents our progression into the Most Holy Place. What happens to our prayers at that point?

_____

_____

_____

(5b.) Is it possible to be a "selfish" intercessor and why?

_____

_____

_____

(5c.) Why is it not permitted to bypass any step or stage in the Tabernacle?

_____

_____

_____

(5d.) What is a familiar zone and who controls it?

_____

_____

_____

(5e.) What three things make up the pattern of God?

_____

_____

_____

(5f.) At what points do you use the Word within this pattern?

_____

_____

_____

Composition Questions

1. Have you continued to read the Bible every day, especially the books of John, Romans, and Genesis? Have you looked up the scriptures that pertain to the areas God wants you to change in your life? Write down in your journal how God has begun to "wash" your life through His Word (start to record your spiritual testimonies).

2. When you read the Word, are there certain scriptures that "stick out" to you? If so, stop and meditate on these verses and find others on the same topic. Write down what you are learning from "searching" God's Word.

3. Are your thoughts and feelings changing about habits, circumstances, and/or people in your life? Is God dealing with you to make some changes? If so, ask Him how you should begin. As He prompts you through this process, write each step down in your journal. Then look back and see if a pattern is developing.

4. Have "traces of wickedness" surfaced within you during this time of washing? If so, let God show you how to deal with it. As they come to the surface, give them to God (in repentance), ask Him to "create a clean heart" in you, and to "renew" your spirit. Forgive yourself. Ask others to forgive you. Confess and be healed. Write your testimony, and then get up and start washing again.

5. Are you starting to see a "new you," as God reflects who you really are through the Brazen Laver? Write down the things He prompts you to do, and record every victory, so that you can trace the pattern and walk in it, over and over again.

6. As you "hold fast your confession," according to Hebrews 4:12–14, are you learning how to speak the Word into your own life? Are you practicing how to say nothing, when you recognize that the words are coming from your earthly nature? Are you learning how to hold the spiritual truths God is teaching you in prayer, until (and if) He tells you to release them? Study about the "tongue" in God's Word. Record your journey.

7. Are you praying every day, at the time God has directed? Are you obeying Him throughout the day, praying whenever He prompts you to pray—even if it is for just a few minutes, or less? Are you ready to surrender your will to God at the Brazen Altar?

Selah

Pause, and Calmly Think of That

MEDITATION

Upon the Completion Of Chapter Three please write your most intimate thoughts about this chapter

_____

_____

_____

_____

_____

_____

_____

_____

_____

_____

_____

_____

_____

Chapter Four
THE BRAZEN ALTAR REVIEW

THE PLACE OF SACRIFICE

Once you have washed at the Brazen Laver, acknowledging everything that God has shown you is displeasing to Him, it is time to be purified at the Brazen Altar. This is the second stage (of the third step in God's pattern of prayer), where you let go of your will, and embrace what God desires. Infant prayer says, "Give me this, give me that." The prayer of sacrifice says, "God, I surrender to your will. Whatever You want, I want. Yes, Lord!"

So, you have entered through the Gate of the works of Jesus Christ with thanksgiving and praise, you have submitted to the "washing of the Word" at the Brazen Laver, and now you know exactly what you look like and what "manner of man" you are. You have come through "the way," but you are still in the realm of personal prayer. You have not gotten to the level of "truth," where you will make intercession for others, because your Outer Court experience is not complete. You must be broken before the Lord.

The Outer Court experience must be "inclusive"— you must pass through every stage—or your prayers will be limited to the realm of the Outer Court, YOU.

WHAT IS AN ALTAR?

The word, "altar," means a "slaughter" place. Strong's 4196 & 2076, Heb. In the Greek, it is called "a place of sacrifice." Strong's 2379, 2378 & 2380 The Brazen Altar is the place where the things of the flesh—bad and good— are burned up by the all-consuming fire of God. It is the stage where you become a "living sacrifice," according to Romans 12:1–3.

"I appeal to you therefore, brethren, and beg of you in view of [all] the mercies of God, to make a decisive dedication of your bodies [presenting all your members and

faculties] as a living sacrifice, holy (devoted, consecrated) and well pleasing to God, which is your reasonable (rational, intelligent) service and spiritual worship. Do not be conformed to this world (this age), [fashioned after and adapted to its external, superficial customs], but be transformed (changed) by the [entire] renewal of your mind [by its new ideals and its new attitude], so that you may prove [for yourselves] what is the good and acceptable and perfect will of God, even the thing which is good and acceptable and perfect [in His sight for you]. For by the grace (unmerited favor of God) given to me I warn everyone among you not to estimate and think of himself more highly than he ought [not to have an exaggerated opinion of his own importance], but to rate his ability with sober judgment, each according to the degree of faith apportioned by God to him."
(AMP)

Remember, you are a priest unto God, a member of the "royal priesthood" of Christ. You must be washed, and you must undergo the fire of consecration. This is the place where you take the "new ideals and attitude" you received at the Brazen Laver to the next level—proving that you will submit to God's perfect will for your life—body, soul, and spirit. Otherwise, how can God use you to make intercession for others?

A SOUND CONSTRUCTION

God told Moses in Exodus 27:1–8,

"And make the altar of acacia wood, five cubits square and three cubits high [within reach of all]. Make horns for it on its four corners; they shall be of one piece with it, and you shall overlay it with bronze. You shall make pots to take away its ashes, and shovels, basins, forks, and firepans; make all its utensils of bronze. Also make for it a grate, a network of bronze; and on the net you shall make four bronze rings at its four corners. And you shall put it under the ledge of the altar, so that the net will extend halfway down the altar. And make poles for the altar, poles of acacia wood overlaid with bronze. The poles shall be put through the rings on the two sides of the altar, with which to carry it. You shall make [the altar] hollow with slabs or planks; as shown you on the mountain, so shall it be made."
(AMP)

Let me encourage you. Five is the number of grace, and three represents the godhead. So when you go to the Brazen Altar, you are submitting to (proving) the work of the godhead…so you will be "transformed" by the grace of God! Though you must come to the Brazen Altar on God's terms, you are by no means alone. Jesus is already in the fire (perfecting it), so He will be with you…just like He was with Shadrach, Meshach, and Abednego. ^{Dan. 3:24–25} (Let me remind you that they were not "consumed" in the fire, and God was with them, because they had refused to serve and worship other gods. ^{Dan. 3:12} We will study this more deeply in the next volume.)

The Brazen Altar was formed out of wood, and   then overlaid in bronze. This means it had to be measured, because wood represents humanity; and whenever humanity is involved, there are limitations. The bronze signifies judgment, so God established the Brazen Altar as the place of blood s a c r i f i c e , where the blood of Christ would make the final atonement for the limitations of man! The priests slaughtered the sacrificial lambs at the Brazen Altar, and Jesus is the Lamb that was slain, according to **Isaiah 53:5–7,**

"But He was wounded for our transgressions, He was bruised for our guilt and iniquities; the chastisement [needful to obtain] peace and well-being for us was upon Him, and with the stripes [that wounded] Him we are healed and made whole. All we like sheep have gone astray, we have turned everyone to his own way; and the Lord has made to light upon Him the guilt and iniquity of us all. He was oppressed, [yet when] He was afflicted, He was submissive and opened not His mouth; like a lamb that is led to the slaughter, and as a sheep before her shearers is dumb, so He opened not His mouth."(AMP)

Questions

1. What Is An Altar?

(1a.) The Altar is a place where u make a decision about your future. The altar must be altered. How should this be done?

_____

_____

_____

(1b.) Why is the fire meant to be continuously?

_____

_____

_____

(1c.) What causes us to have empty worship?

_____

_____

_____

2. A Sound Construction

(2a.)The bronze altar was used for sacrifice. What was on the four corners of the altar?

_____

_____

_____

(2b.) What was their purpose? (also see Psalm 118:27)

_____

_____

_____

3. An Equal Sacrifice

(3a.) What are the dimensions of the Brazen Altar?

_____

_____

_____

(3b.) Based on the book what is the symbolic meaning as it relates to our sacrifice?

_____

_____

_____

(3c.) Does your sacrifice determine your authority in prayer? Why?

_____

_____

_____

(3d.) By applying the means of the altar, what type of light is made available to us?

_____

_____

_____

(3e.) According to Lev. 9:23-24, how many days did Moses and Aaron spend in consecration?

_____

_____

_____

(3f.) What was the purpose of this consecration? What were they in pursuit of?

_____

_____

_____

(3g.) Where did the original flame that sat upon the altar originate from? Why is it important that they could not start this fire? Could the fire ever go out?

_____

_____

_____

4.The Horns Of Help

(4a.)In Luke 1:68-69 what was praising God for and what else was he doing in theses verses?

_____

_____

_____

(4b.) What do the Horns represent? (please provide scripture reference)

_____

_____

_____

5.Beware Of Strange Fire

(5a.) What causes us people to operate in "strange fire"?

_____

_____

_____

(5b.) What was the reason for the death of Aaron's sons? (Lev. 10:1-3)

_____

_____

_____

6. A Final Warning

(6a.)When the sun of the natural light goes down, what is the only light that remains?

_____

_____

_____

(6b.) When is it the right time to rise up from the altar? How will you know?

_____

_____

Questions Continued

1 What is the 2ⁿᵈ stage of the Brazen Laver?

_____

_____

_____

2 At the 2ⁿᵈ stage, of the 3ʳᵈ step in God's prayer pattern, there are two imperative acts that must be done while moving forward in this prayer journey. Please list them?

(a.) _____

(b.) _____

3 Define the word "Altar" and please provide scripture reference for the definition?

_____

_____

_____

4 When approaching the Brazen Altar, we should follow the example of Jesus as He endured the crucifixion. What personal act should we perfect when approaching the Brazen Altar; Jesus was our perfect example?

_____

_____

_____

5 There are a series of things that happen when you put yourself on the Brazen Altar, letting go of your will. Describe a few of these things which take place, that are discussed in this chapter?

_____

_____

_____

Composition Questions
The Brazen Laver The Place of Washing Ex. 30:19–21

Have you continued to read the Bible every day, especially the books of John, Romans, and Genesis? Have you looked up the scriptures that pertain to the areas God wants you to change in your life? Write down in your journal how God has begun to "wash" your life through His Word (start to record your spiritual testimonies).

When you read the Word, are there certain scriptures that "stick out" to you? If so, stop and meditate on these verses and find others on the same topic. Write down what you are learning from "searching" God's Word

.

Are your thoughts and feelings changing about habits, circumstances, and/or people in your life? Is God dealing with you to make some changes? If so, ask Him how you should begin. As He prompts you through this process, write each step down in your journal. Then look back and see if a pattern is developing.

Have "traces of wickedness" surfaced within you during this time of washing? If so, let God show you how to deal with it. As they come to the surface, give them to God (in repentance), ask Him to "create a clean heart" in you, and to "renew" your spirit. Forgive yourself. Ask others to forgive you. Confess and be healed. Write your testimony, and then get up and start washing again.

Are you starting to see a "new you," as God reflects who you really are through the Brazen Laver? Write down the things He prompts you to do, and record every victory, so that you can trace the pattern and walk in it, over and over again.

Are you praying every day, at the time God has directed? Are you obeying Him throughout the day, praying whenever He prompts you to pray—even if it is for just a few minutes, or less? Are you ready to surrender your will to God at the Brazen Altar?

Selah

Pause, and Calmly Think of That   MEDITATION

Upon the Completion of Chapter Four please write your most intimate thoughts about this chapter

_____

_____

_____

_____

_____

_____

_____

_____

_____

_____

_____

_____

Chapter Five
THE PRIEST'S CLOTHING REVIEW

(NOTE: Because of the intensity of this chapter, I felt lead to lead to place all of the introduction in this chapter in this section of the workbook.)

PREPARING TO ENTER THE HOLY PLACE

Moses, whom God had chosen to lead His people out of Egypt, was working with **"the flock of Jethro his father in law, the priest of Midian..."** He had led them **"from the backside of the desert, and came to the mountain of God." Exodus 3:1.** This is significant to our walk of prayer. To me, it marked the spiritual birthing of Moses' Tabernacle in the wilderness...our pattern of prayer from the "finished work"—the physical Tabernacle—which was constructed in the book of Exodus.

Remember what I said about the "completed harvest" at the end of the Preface? To conclude this volume of the series, God is taking us back to our beginnings. Why? Like I said in the beginning, with God everything is already "finished." You are now about to enter into the "harvest" of His finished work in the Outer Court. You have come to the third and final stage in step 3 of God's pattern of prayer. You have "followed" His pattern to "completed" salvation, and divine preparation to move to the next level...the Holy Place.

Let us continue reading about Moses,

"And the angel of the Lord appeared unto him in a flame of fire out of the midst of the bush: and he looked, and, behold, the bush burned with fire, and the bush was not consumed. And Moses said, I will now turn aside, and see this great sight, why the bush is not burnt. And when the Lord saw that he turned aside to see, God called unto him out of the midst of the bush, and said, Moses, Moses. And he said, Here am I. And he said, Draw not nigh hither: put off thy shoes from off thy feet, for the place where on thou standest is holy ground. Moreover he said, I

am the God of thy father, the God of Abraham, the God of Isaac, and the God of Jacob. And Moses hid his face; for he was afraid to look upon God. And the Lord said, I have surely seen the affliction of my people which are in Egypt, and have heard their cry by reason of their taskmasters; for I know their sorrows; and I am come down to deliver them out of the hand of the Egyptians, and to bring them up out of that land unto a good land and a large, unto a land flowing with milk and honey…Come now therefore; and I will send thee unto Pharaoh, that thou mayest bring forth my people the children of Israel out of Egypt."
Exodus 3:2-8 &10

First of all, the "burning bush" was not consumed because God was in the midst of it. It was a manifestation of the fire that came down from heaven and lit the Brazen Altar! God is perfect, so the bush was not consumed. So the "bush" in this passage is a "type" of the perfect fire from the third dimension, but also the cleansing fire on the altar of sacrifice—and it symbolizes the "fires" that will burn in the second and third realms of prayer (which I will be covering in volumes II and III). Stay with me. *The best is yet to come.*

Moses had to take off his shoes, his natural means o f transportation, before God could speak to him from within the fire, and give him new direction. In prayer, after God gets you off of the Brazen Altar, then and only then, are you able to receive new direction from heaven…and begin to be clothed by the Spirit of God. This is also a warning— though the Brazen Altar is hot— extremely uncomfortable, to the extent that you want to jump off and run, it is a holy place (I will get to this shortly). It is the place of divine "appointment." Having "completed" this level of your salvation at the altar—the final destination of Outer Court Christianity—your life is about to change—forever.

Then something powerful happened, "…Moses hid his face, for he was afraid to look upon God." **Proverbs 1:7** says, **"The reverent and worshipful fear of the Lord is the beginning and the principal and choice part of knowledge [its starting point and its essence]; but fools despise skillful and godly Wisdom, instruction, and discipline."** (AMP) In other words, before you get off of the Brazen Altar (as I said before), you may have knowledge of the Word, but you do not yet have divine revelation…because you must fear God before you can hear from Him, and you must hear from God to serve Him. So God confirmed His pattern to

Moses…

"…I am the God of thy father, the God of Abraham, the God of Isaac, and the God of Jacob." Exodus 3:6, (AMP)

In other words, He was saying, "I am the God who gave My Word to your fathers. They learned to walk out My revealed Word, and so will you. Their pattern is your pattern. Your life is getting ready to change." This is why we have to experience the first manifestation of "the burning bush" at the Brazen Altar, so that, according to the words of Solomon,

"That people [you] may know skillful and godly Wisdom and instruction, discern and comprehend the words of understanding and insight, receive instruction in wise dealing and the discipline of wise thoughtfulness, righteousness, justice, and integrity, that prudence may be given to the simple, and knowledge, discretion, and discernment to the youth—the wise also will hear and increase in learning, and the person of understanding will acquire skill and attain to sound counsel [so that he may be able to steer his course rightly]—that people may understand a proverb and a figure of speech or an enigma with its interpretation, and the words of the wise and their dark sayings or riddles." Proverbs 1:2–6, (AMP)

Questions

1. The summary of the dimensions

(1a.) What is this stage of the process called? Explain why/

_____

_____

_____

1b.)   Name two attributes of the burning bush and its fire.

_____

_____

_____

(1c.) Why was Moses asked to remove His shoes?

_____

_____

_____

(1d.) Why did Moses hide his face from God?

_____

_____

_____

(1e.) Explain in your own words the meaning of Proverbs 1:7

_____

_____

_____

(1f.) Explain why He was the God of each of them and how that should apply to your life?

_____

_____

_____

(1g.) According to Proverbs 1:2-6, What is God's purpose I doing this?

_____

_____

_____

For every explanation written, go to the dictionary and write the meaning of each one.

_____

_____

_____

_____

_____

_____

_____

_____

_____

_____

_____

_____

_____

_____

_____

_____

_____

_____

_____

_____

_____

_____

_____

_____

_____

2. The Tunic

(2a.) According to Lev 8:7, what color was the tunic? Why was this color chosen?

_____

_____

_____

(2b.) What part of the Tabernacle matched the tunic?

_____

_____

_____

(2c.) What did this represent?

_____

_____

_____

(2d.) According to Exodus 28:42-43, what is the second piece of garment made of, and what was the purpose?

_____

_____

_____

(2e.) What was the difference between the way Aaron wore the tunic and the say his sons wore them? Described why.

_____

_____

_____

(2f.) According to 2 Peter 1:1-8, when our nature is submitted to the righteousness of God, what are seven things we are to pursue with all diligence?

_____

_____

_____

3.The Girdle

(3a.) What is another name for girdle?

_____

_____

_____

(3b.) Why is it worn where no one can see it?

_____

_____

_____

(3c.) What did the hidden girdle represent?

_____

_____

_____

(3d.) According to Isaiah 11:4-5, how does the sash assist in long hours of prayer?

_____

_____

_____

(3e.) According to Ephesians 6:14, name the two functions of the sash/girdle.

_____

_____

_____

4. The Robe

(4a.) Describe the robe.

_____

_____

_____

(4b.) What color was it, and what was the meaning of this color?

_____

_____

_____

(4c.) What did the hidden girdle represent?

_____

_____

_____

(4d.) Why was the robe adorned with tassels of 72 bells?

_____

_____

_____

(4e.) Why were there pomegranates on the robe?

_____

_____

_____

(4f.) Why were there 72 bells and 72 pomegranates?

_____

_____

_____

5. The Ephod

(5a.) What was the significance of the Ephod?

_____

_____

_____

(5b.) When was this piece worn?

_____

_____

_____

(5c.) Name the colors and their meanings. How were they held together?

_____

_____

_____

(5d.) Why was it necessary for the gold cord that held the ephod together be beaten out?

_____

_____

_____

(5e.) What type of stones were on the shoulders of the ephod?

_____

_____

_____

6. The Breastplate

(6a.) The breastplate was also known to be the breastplate of

_____

_____

_____

(Exo. 28:15-30)

(6b.) What did it represent?

_____

_____

_____

(6c.) How many stones were on the breastplate?

_____

_____

_____

(6d.) What did they represent?

_____

_____

_____

(6e.) How many inches was the breastplate?

_____

_____

_____

(6f.) Name the two items placed inside the breastplate.

_____

_____

_____

(6g.) Why did the priests place their hands on these two items?

_____

_____

_____

6h.) **What was written on the parchment, which was also inside the breastplate?**

_____

_____

_____

6i.) **What does Urim mean?**

_____

_____

_____

6j.) **What does Thummim mean?**

_____

_____

_____

6k.) **As it relates to the Urim and the Thummim, what would happen to the individual letters as a result of these two actions?**

_____

_____

_____

6l.) **Why is the breastplate referred to as a prayer list?**

_____

_____

_____

7. The Mitre

(7a.) Describe the Mitre, including its other name? What is the meaning? What part of the body was the Mitre on?

_____

_____

_____

(7b.) What was attached to the Mitre? According to Ephesians 4:1-3, what is the Mitre likened to?

_____

_____

_____

(7c.) This Mitre was a reminder to priests to always conduct themselves how? And why?

_____

_____

_____

You Are A Living Tabernacle

1. Now that you know who you are, share your narrative of it life looks likes as a "Living Tabernacle"?

_____

_____

_____

2. When the priest would put on their clothing, what did it represent?

_____

_____

_____

3.What was the intended reflection of their garments to represent?

_____

_____

_____

4. What type of glory was upon them because of the garments?

_____

_____

_____

5. According to 2 Cor 6:16 who have we become?

_____

_____

_____

6. In looking back at the garments, can you find an identification of each one in your life? If not, explain what is missing. How do you plan to have your tabernacle become a reflection of the Tabernacle of Moses?

_____

_____

_____

Questions Continued

(These questions are constructed for open discussions)

According to Exodus 3:1, what marks the spiritual birthing of Moses' Tabernacle in the wilderness? And, what is its significance to our prayer walk?

_____

_____

_____

This chapter represents the entrance into the final stage of step 3. What does the book call this stage?

_____

_____

_____

In Exodus 3, the "Burning Bush" event is a clear depiction of the Miracle working power of God. Explain why this event is significant to the Brazen Altar?

_____

_____

_____

The Brazen Altar is described as hot, and extremely uncomfortable…
Yet, it is a place of

_____

_____

The and fear of the Lord is _____

he beginning and the and _____

part of _____

_____

(Prov. 1:7 AMP)

You have been *cleansed* through the Word, by way of prayer at the

_____

_____

_____

You have been purified through the sacrificial prayer at the

_____

_____

_____

What does the book say are the enemies of your faith with a God that answers Prayer?

_____

_____

_____

Composition Questions
The Priest's Clothing

Have you ever had a "burning bush" experience with God? Are you beginning to discern His presence more accurately now that He has taken you off of the Brazen Altar? What is being birthed in your spirit as He dresses you to enter the Holy Place of intercession? Write it down.

Are you beginning to receive insight an understanding of God's Word on a deeper level? Look back through your Bible study notes, and journal, and record these new revelations. Begin to ask God what He wants you to do as you prepare to serve Him in the Holy Place. Write down His reply.

Examine your life. Can you look in the mirror of God's Word and see your new tunic of righteousness? Have you become a "doer" of the Word, consistently? Write down the areas where God has given you the greatest testimonies

Are your loins "girded" with your priestly sash? Are you using it faithfully, whenever you need the strength of the Lord? Record these experiences in your journal

Are you beginning to experience new power in prayer? Is your robe of divine authority equally balanced with the fruit of righteousness, and your spiritual gifts? Write a list of your godly character traits, alongside of your spiritual gifts. Is there a balance? If not, address areas that are lacking through prayer—and then wash, sacrifice, and start the list again.

Do you keep the 4 works of Christ girded to your ephod? Have you endured in prayer to the point that Christ will come and take over, leading you in intercession? Are you walking in humility, toward God and man? Journal your progress.

Is your breastplate securely fastened? Who is God putting on your heart to carry into the place of prayer? Write their names on your prayer list and begin to ask God to lead you in prayer on their behalf. Be available if they need you, always lead them to God, and do everything in Jesus' name.

Is your breastplate securely fastened? Who is God putting on your heart to carry into the place of prayer? Write their names on your prayer list and begin to ask God to lead you in prayer on their behalf. Be available if they need you, always lead them to God, and do everything in Jesus' name.

Selah

Pause, and Calmly Think of That

MEDITATION

Upon the Completion of Chapter Five please write your most intimate thoughts about this chapter

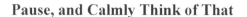

_____

_____

_____

_____

_____

_____

_____

_____

_____

_____

_____

_____

_____

_____

_____

Dear Reader,

I would like to take this time to thank you for your interest in my literary works. I pray that you were tremendously blessed by the study of this book, and that you would continue in your pursuit after a higher dimension in God. I invite you to join me on Facebook for my live program entitled "@3 With Me" at 3pm EST, Monday through Wednesday. There, you will receive live, extensive teachings on the subject of prayer. Also, connect with me on Impact TV, which airs on Comcast/DirecTV. Follow me on Facebook @iamdrjuanitabynum and on Periscope @iamdrjuanitabynum, as well as visiting me on my website,
www.juanitabynum.com

May the Lord richly bless you…
Signed,
Dr. Juanita Bynum

Other literary works available

Dr. Juanita Bynum
𝔑𝔢𝔴 𝔜𝔬𝔯𝔨 𝔗𝔦𝔪𝔢𝔰 **Bestselling Author**

Praying From The Third Dimension
(Book and Workbook)
The Juanita Bynum Topical
The Threshing Floor
Matters of The Heart

No More Sheets
My Spiritual Inheritance
Don't Get Off The Train
The Planted Seed

40868783R00075

Made in the USA
Middletown, DE
25 February 2017